First edition for the United States and Canada published
in 2008 by Barron's Educational Series, Inc.

First edition of *I Think I Am Going to Sneeze*
first published for Great Britain in 2008 by Wayland,
a division of Hachette Children's Books

All inquiries should be addressed to:
Barron's Educational Series, Inc.
250 Wireless Boulevard
Hauppauge, New York 11788
www.barronseduc.com

Library of Congress Control Number: 2008926684

ISBN-13: 978-0-7641-3900-0
ISBN-10: 0-7641-3900-2

Printed in China
9 8 7 6 5 4 3 2 1

Disclaimer
The Web site addresses (URLs) included in this book were
valid at the time of going to press. However, because of
the nature of the Internet, it is possible that some addresses
may have changed, or sites may have changed or closed
down since publication. While the publisher regrets any
inconvenience this may cause readers, no responsibility for
any such changes will be accepted by the publisher.

I Think I Am Going to Sneeze

A FIRST LOOK AT ALLERGIES

PAT THOMAS
ILLUSTRATED BY LESLEY HARKER

BARRON'S

Your nose gets tingly, your eyes get watery, your throat gets scratchy, and your skin gets itchy.

Sometimes it can feel like
your body has gone crazy.

Most people feel like this only when they get a cold.

But if you have allergies you might feel like this often.

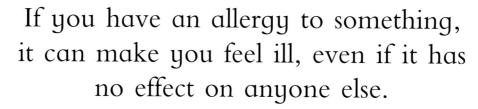

If you have an allergy to something,
it can make you feel ill, even if it has
no effect on anyone else.

An allergy gives you uncomfortable
feelings (or symptoms)—like itchy
skin—when your body thinks
it has come into contact
with something harmful.

Allergies can be passed
from parents to children,
but not everyone reacts
in the same way or to
the same things.

So even if your mom gets a runny nose when she's allergic to something, you might not. Instead, you might get watery eyes or a scratchy throat.

What about you?

Does anyone in your family or anyone else you know have an allergy? Do you know what they are allergic to?

Allergies can be caused by lots
of different things. They can be
caused by things in the air like
dust, or pollen from trees and grass.

They can be caused by things you eat,
like nuts, milk, or wheat in bread and cakes.
Fish, shellfish, or the flavors in snack foods
can also be causes of allergies.

Allergies can be
caused by touching
or being near pets
like cats and dogs.
Birds can sometimes
cause allergies, too.

You can also be allergic to insects, such as dust mites, and to bee or wasp stings.

What about you?

Do you have an allergy?

Do you know what you are allergic to?

If you have an allergy, your body thinks that whatever is causing it is something bad, so it tries to fight back.

Symptoms of an allergy, such as a sneeze or a cough, are the result of your body's fight with the cause of the allergy.

When you first get an allergy you may
not know what is causing it. For some children,
the symptoms can be so bad that they need
to go to the hospital to get better.

That can be really scary. But your family and your doctor will make sure you are safe and that you get well as soon as possible.

Your doctor can help by giving you some medicine to make the symptoms go away.

He can also do special tests on your skin or your blood that can help find out what you are allergic to.

Once you know what you are allergic to, you can learn how to avoid it. Your family, friends, and teachers will help you do this.

And the good news is that as you get older there is a chance your allergy will go away. For example, many children grow out of allergies to milk and wheat.

Sometimes having an allergy means
giving up things that you really like.
And sometimes that can be
frustrating and make you
feel left out.

But don't worry. With a little extra care, you can enjoy all the fun things everyone else enjoys.

HOW TO USE THIS BOOK

When you talk to your child about health, it's best to be honest, open, and positive. Tell your child that although allergies can't be cured, he or she can stop the worst of the symptoms by avoiding whatever is causing the allergy. Also, many children outgrow allergies as they get older.

Very young children will not fully understand their condition and cannot be in complete control of their choices or environments in order to avoid all allergy triggers. They won't have the forethought required to make the link between potential allergens and feeling bad, and they may still expose themselves to triggers and risks if they are part of a group or if the activity looks fun. Until the child develops this faculty, family, friends, and teachers will have to be patient and vigilant to help the child avoid potential allergens, such as by removing potential allergens from the home.

Although food allergies remain among the most common types of allergies, anyone can be allergic to almost anything. Medical tests can help get to the bottom of what is causing the allergy, but equally, an allergy test can prove negative even when the child is clearly reacting to a specific food. If you are convinced your child is allergic to a food but the test is negative, visit an allergist for further testing.

Different children react to living with allergies differently. It's important to tailor your approach to your own child and provide the right level of reassurance and empathy. As often as possible, help your child understand that while allergies can't be ignored, he or she can live a normal life. While your child is coming to terms with his or her allergy, encourage descriptive, feeling words to describe symptoms. As early as you can, make sure your child learns to recognize the things that trigger an allergic reaction, and reinforce the need to avoid these things. Also, make sure your child knows about any medications he or she might need. Allergy medications come in a variety of forms, such as sprays, pumps, pills, and creams.

Communication with caregivers and teachers is also important. If your child has an allergy you will need to work with other significant adults so that everyone knows what triggers to avoid and what to do if the child is accidentally exposed to an allergen. Make sure you are aware of any planned activities that might involve exposure to significant allergens.

Young children who suffer an extreme allergic reaction that leads to anaphylaxis (severely, potentially fatal, restricted breathing and swollen throat) may need to carry an EpiPen or Twinject with them. This gives an emergency injection of a substance called epinephrine (otherwise know as adrenaline). Make sure teachers and caregivers know where this item is kept and how to use it.

In school, learning about allergies can be covered through health education (how the lungs work and what allergies are, for instance) and also through science (e.g., understanding environmental triggers such as pollen). Many students may have experience with their own allergies or have a family member or friend who is allergic to something. Talking openly in a group setting about allergies and the things that cause them can help children feel more at ease with their condition.

BOOKS TO READ

Allie the Allergic Elephant: A Children's Story of Peanut Allergies
Nicole Smith (Allergic Child Publishing Group, 2006)

A Day at the Playground with Food Allergies
Tracie Schrand (Llumina Kids, 2006)

Zooallergy: A Fun Story About Allergy and Asthma Triggers
Kim Gosselin (Jayjo Books, 1996)

Aaron's Awful Allergies
Troon Harrison and Eugenie Fernandes
(Kids Can Press, Ltd., 1996)

RESOURCES FOR ADULTS

American Academy of Allergy, Asthma, & Immunology
555 East Wells Street
Suite 100
Milwaukee, WI 53202-3823
(414) 272-6071
Patient Information and Physician Referral:
   1-800-822-2762
www.aaai.org

American College of Asthma, Allergy, and Immunology
85 West Algonquin Road, Suite 550
Arlington Heights, IL 60005
Phone: (847) 427-1200
Fax: (847) 427-1294
E-mail: mail@acaai.org
http://www.acaai.org/public/advice/chldrn.htm

*i*Village (A parenting message board)
http://messageboards.ivillage.com/iv-ppallergies

Asthma and Allergy Foundation of America
1233 20th Street, NW
Suite 402
Washington, DC 20036
Hotline: 1-800-7-ASTHMA (1-800-727-8462)
www.aafa.org

Canadian Health Network
http://www.canadian-health-network.ca

Blue Bear Aware (an allergy resource network)
839 Burnaby Street
New Westminster
BC, Canada V3L 4V8
Phone: (604) 760-5573
E-mail: info@bluebearaware.com
www.bluebearaware.com

BOOKS

Beyond a Peanut: Is This Safe? (Ring-bound) Dina Clifford (Mind Flight LL, 2007)

Understanding and Managing Your Child's Food Allergies Scott H. Sicherer (The Johns Hopkins University Press, 2006)

Is This Your Child? Doris Rapp (Harper Paperbacks, 1992)